BISHOPSTON

1. Cheltenham Road looking from the Arches towards Zetland Road Junction, showing the shop of J.H. Mills Ltd. which in later years was to become the Gateway Supermarket.

2. Looking in the opposite direction to the above picture. A superb photographic card, showing a man selling flowers from a basket, a hand cart, a horse and cart from which manure is being sold, and trams. Both publisher and photographer unknown.

BISHOPSTON

3. Elton Road connecting Zetland Road Junction. Tyne Path, which once was a very early right of way for travellers to Horfield, and on out to Aust. Card published by Viner.

4. Zetland Road Junction, with Elton Road off to the left. Just in view, the milkman delivering milk from a churn, tram no. 189 travelling toward Ashley Down, whilst the other is about to depart for Staple Hill. Card postally used 1914.

BISHOPSTON

5. Zetland Road leading to Redland, with Cheltenham Road to the left. The shop on the right S.T. Pont, supplier of English and Italian Provisions. This card posted in 1903.

6. Zetland Road Tramway Junction. Looking towards the main Gloucester Road, the tram shelter at the corner of Elton Road, with tram lines criss-crossing from four directions, the Bishopston Branch of the Bristol Tramways and Carriage Company. In later years became shops. This view 1905.

7. Gloucester Road. The selection of shops much the same in this view in the 1950's. The large houses on the left of picture 4, converted to shops.

8. Gloucester Road at the junction with Raglan Road, showing the Post Office, and Off Licence. The shops opposite include Singers Sewing Machines, C.E. Longstaff Bazaar, and E.W. Crouch. Published by Viner.

9. Belmont Road looking towards the David Thomas Memorial Church, now turned into flats. A very quiet scene, perhaps a Sunday morning. Card postally used 1909.

10. Berkeley Road looking down towards the Gloucester Road, with Somerville Road beyond. Card published by Brightman, Redland Road. Postally used 1908.

11. North Road looking towards the bottom of Somerville Road, with St. Michaels and All Angels Church in the distance.

12. North Road looking the opposite way to the above picture, almost at the junction of Overton Road.

13. Gloucester Road. Bristol North Baths are on the right of the picture, with the old Horfield Inn next door, trading today under the new name The Bristol Flyer. Postcard published by W.H. Smith in their Grosvenor Series.

14. Gloucester Road. The Bishopston Methodist Chapel on the corner of Berkeley Road opened in 1865 and closed in 1960, the tower now removed, and is now a car tyre business. Shops include Mitchells Fishmonger. Card posted July 1913.

15. Gloucester Road. An early view showing the Horfield Inn, now The Bristol Flyer. The houses with front gardens before conversion to shops. Card postally used in 1911.

16. Looking up a tree lined view of Gloucester Road, at the junction with Somerville Road, on the right Henry Hodder Chemist, and shops extend to bottom of the hill, known locally as "Pigsty Hill".

17. Wolseley Road. Between Broadway Road and Gloucester Road, named after Garnet Joseph Viscount Wolseley (1833-1913). Postcard posted in 1916 and published by Brightman of Redland.

18. Shadwell Road running parallel with Wolseley Road from Gloucester Road, with different architecture, and also showing distant view of St. Andrews. Named after Julius Shadwell, one of the Lords of the Manor of Horfield. Card published by Kelly and Harvey, 58, Gloucester Road.

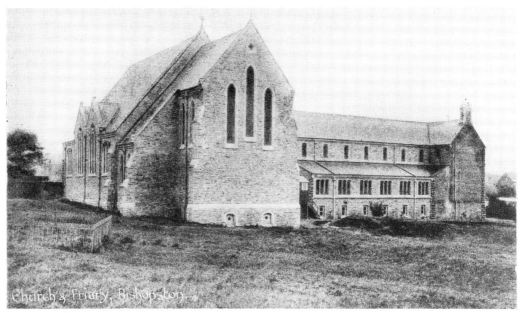

19. In 1889 agreement was reached with the Shadwell Trustees, who owned much of the land in the Logan and Shadwell Road area, which was originally part of Shadwell Farm, to purchase land to build a Friary. Three and a half acres of land was purchased at the top of Egerton Road. This Franciscan Friary and Church known as St. Bonaventures.

20. The interior of the church. St. Bonaventures School adjoins the church and friary at the top of Egerton Road, the old school was replaced by a modern building in recent years.

Somerville Road and Berkerley Road Bishopston   Bristol

21. Somerville Road from the top of the hill looking down to Gloucester Road. The houses were large and varied in design, most of which were built in the late 1890's. Card posted in 1907.

22. Somerville Road. This view of the houses at the top end were built after Egerton and Berkeley Roads, attracting business people moving out from the city. Card posted in May 1905.

23. Egerton Road looking towards the friary and church of St. Bonaventures, with Dulverton Road the turning off on middle right of the picture.

24. Egerton Road looking in the opposite direction towards Gloucester Road. The card sent from 110 Egerton Road, in November 1907.

25. Broadway Road, a long tree lined road connecting Tyne Road with Berkeley Road. Card postally used in 1907.

26. Hazleton Road built on land purchased from Hazleton Farm, it is a turning off Broadway Road. Postcard sent from Bristol in April 1916. Published by Viners of Bath.

27. Logan Road looking towards the turning with Claremont Road on the right. Probably named after the Rev. J. Moffat Logan, who held discussion classes for many years in Upper Cheltenham Place. Card by Brightman of Redland. Posted in 1913.

28. Logan Road, the opposite direction towards Birchill Road and Kings Drive of today. It was still open fields in 1913, when this card was posted. Both cards published by Brightman of Redland. Again posted in 1913.

29. St. Michaels and All Angels. The church consecrated in 1862 and later extended in 1878, when the South Transept and Chancel were built. In 1891 the North Aisle was added.

30. St. Michaels and All Angels. An interior view looking up the main aisle to the alter. Card posted in 1913.

31. Bishopston Parish Hall. The foundation stone was layed by Mrs. G.A. Gibbs on September 11th 1907, the hall was built behind the Church of England Schoolroom. Designed by H. Smith, Architect, of 23, Clare Street, Bristol.

32. Hatherley Road from Falmouth Road towards the main Gloucester Road in 1907, named after William Page Wood, Baron Hatherley (1801-81) a distinguished judge. Published locally by Kelly and Harvey, 58, Gloucester Road.

33. Gloucester Road at the top of "Pigsty Hill" looking towards the city with Wesley Road off left, and the Off Licence on the corner of Hatherley Road. Published by Viners of Bath.

34. Gloucester Road Bishopston Methodist Church on the corner of Wesley Road. The houses beyond are mostly private residences, with the towers of Horfield Baptist Church in the distance, tram wires overhead and a distant view of a tram. Published by Viners of Bath.

35. Melbourne Road from Monk Road looking towards St. Michaels Church Halls in the distance. Children standing for the camera. Note the box on wheels, with the group of children on the left. Card not postally used, but taken about 1908.

36. Monmouth Road parallel with Melbourne Road, off Monk Road to Falmouth Road. Houses with bay windows, a milk cart delivering from milk churns, a winter scene with a shower of snow and ice on roof and pavement. Picture taken by a Mr. Brock who lived in Monmouth Road, who used the card to send birthday greetings.

BISHOPSTON

37. Kent Road, one of several around the Gloucestershire County Cricket Ground. Named after County Cricket teams. Published by Brightman of Redland, and posted in 1907.

38. Lancashire Road looking towards Kent Road. The houses on the right back onto the Gloucestershire County Cricket Ground. Again another card by Brightman, posted in 1907.

39. Seymour Avenue connects with Dongola Road and named after the builder. A horse and cart delivering coal, with two small boys standing in the road. Posted in 1909, and published by local photographer Kelly and Harvey of Gloucester Road.

40. Brynland Avenue, a long road which extends from Gloucester Road by St. Michaels Church, to Ashley Down Road. This view taken about half way along towards Dongola Avenue. The name Bryn being Welsh for "Hill". Postally used in 1909. Published by Brightman of Redland.

41. Seymour Road between Nevil Road and Ashley Down Road. The terraced houses on the right with small gardens, with some detached houses opposite back from the road. Card posted in Bristol in 1907.

42. Nevil Road. The County Ground Hotel on the left, by the turning for Dongola Road, in the distance the entrance to Gloucestershire County Cricket Ground. The man holding a tripod for his camera on a summers day. About 1908. Card again by Brightman of Redland.

43. Nevil Road. The County Ground Hotel looking towards the Gloucester Road, The road named after the owner of the land M.H. Nevil Story Maskelyne (1823-1911) Lord of the Manor of Horfield.

44. Gloucestershire County Cricket Ground, the Cricket Pavilion backing onto Lancashire Road. The card says Gloucester batting, but we don't know who they were playing against, or indeed who won!

45. Morley Square. The houses facing their own private gardens, named after Samuel Morley (1809-1885) Member of Parliament for Bristol 1865-1885. The statue to his memory stands at the Horsefair Bristol.

46. Morley Square. A coach outing for the residents, parked outside the houses of the square on the south side. Coach hired from Bristol Tramway and Carriage Co. Ltd. in the early 1920's. Published by Garratt.

47. Bishopston outing to Blaise Castle, when it was still owned by the Harford family. Card published by Garratt, and taken about 1908.

48. Gloucester Road on the corner of Nevil Road in 1907. The corner shop is still a chemist, the iron railings have gone, now there is a walled garden with a wooden gate, a distant view of Horfield Baptist Church before the wooden towers were removed.

49. Falmouth Road looking towards Horfield Prison in the middle distance. The turning on the left is Monmouth Road. Card published by Brightman 1906.

50. Manor Road. This view looking towards Hatherley Road from Bishop Road. Card posted in 1906. There was never a Manor of Bishopston, but the road takes it's name from Horfield Manor, as they once owned the land.

51. Gloucester Road looking towards the centre of the city. Horfield Baptist Church was built in 1900, after earlier meetings were held in Thornleigh Road, Horfield, formed by a group from Broadmead Chapel. Shops on the right still a busy shopping area today.

52. Gloucester Road looking in the opposite direction with a closer view of the many shops, Crawford's Newsagents on the left, with the Dairy opposite.

53. Bishop Road School situated in the road of that name, and the corner of Cambridge Road. It was opened in 1890's, and consisted of infant, junior and senior schools.

54. A group of girls in the 1930's when girls and boys were in separate schools, taken in the playground adjoining Bishop Road. The teacher on the right is Miss Franklin who taught mainly geography at the school until she retired.

55. Gloucester Road, Bishopston. This card looking north from Longmead Avenue and Nevil Road, Lloyds Bank and Anchor Inn showing in the middle distance. Pearces Ironmongers on the right, still trading today.

56. The same view taken slightly further back, shows the large house on the corner of Nevil Road. The card was posted in 1923. The Conservative Club was built on the corner when the two houses were demolished. Note the confusion between the publisher's where the border of Bishopston and Horfield starts and finishes, still a source of many arguments today.

57. Gloucester Road between the bottom of Bishop Road and Cambridge Road, showing the Golden Lion Hotel and the shops adjoining. The upper part of the shops architecture still the same today. Horse and cart waiting outside of J. Trobridge Baker and Cornfactor. Card posted in 1907.

58. Gloucester Road between Nevil Road and Dongola Avenue. The first shop on the right, the ironmongers, owned then by Jewel, now Pearce's, with the public house The Old Fox two doors up. This was the site of Wades Yard in the 1880's. Card posted on July 4th 1907.

59. Gloucester Road, Horfield looking north, on the corner with Ash Road, off to the left. Tram no. 51 travelling down the Gloucester Road with soldiers sitting on top, passing the Royal Oak Inn.

60. Ashley Down Road at its junction with the main Gloucester Road. This view taken in 1913, still mainly unchanged today. In the middle distance the junction with Downend Road. The first shop in the rank selling oil, soap, and candles.

61. Horfield Tram Depot about 1910, this depot was opened in 1892. Tram no. 55 with driver, and tram no. 41 parked to complete the photo. A sign above the conductor, standing on the pavement, reads Blue Motor Taxicabs may be ordered from within without charge. Telephone 335.

62. Gloucester Road at the turning with Church Road, showing the early tram stop sign with its ornate ironwork. The Horfield Tram Depot just above on the left before the Victoria Inn. The card about 1908, published by Garratt.

63. Churchways Avenue looking down to the main Gloucester Road, the road to the right by the small girl, Churchways Crescent. The distant fields of Lockleaze and Purdown clearly seen, Strathmore Road just visible on the bottom right. Postcard sent to London in May 1907.

64. Quarrinton Road built in the same period, the early 1900's, as picture 63, but this picture taken in 1912. This view taken from its junction with Downend Road, looking up towards the main Gloucester Road.

65. Gloucester Road looking towards the city, with Beaufort Road the turning on the left, tram no. 65 en route for Filton, many telegraph poles connecting Bristol to Gloucester telephone exchange, trunk lines opened in 1887. Postcard published by Garratt.

66. Gloucester Road, the junction with Wellington Hill left, and the wide thoroughfare of Filton Avenue to the right of the group of boys, architecturally unchanged, but today a very busy junction controlled by traffic lights.

67. Wellington Hill looking up left from the main road, when the approach led to fields. The sign advertises for the building of houses, to sell or to let, the road to the left continues as Wellington Hill. Card postally used in 1908.

68. Wellington Hill, the continuing road to the left of picture 67, then facing open fields, houses were built including Rosling Road in later years. The postcard was posted in 1906.

69. Horfield Castle formerly known as Lambert House, looking towards the Grammar School playing fields and showing their pavilion in 1910. The house was not strictly a "castle" but the garden wall had a turret effect, with small slits inserted. The wall still shows today, although a modern house has since been built on the land.

70. The Ardagh in the centre of Horfield Common, named after a house formally known as the Poplars, but named Ardagh on a local map of 1903. Today the pavilion is used for many sporting activities including tennis and bowls, with the surrounding grounds well maintained.

71. Horfield Common. Horfield Church of England School, with the Parish Church behind. This card by Garratt taken before 1921, when Kellaway Avenue and Wellington Hill West were constructed.

72. Kellaway Avenue opened by the Postmaster-General Mr. F.G. Kellaway M.P. on 23rd November 1920. This view looking towards Gloucester Road, St. Ann's Cottages on the left, and through the trees, the Ship Inn, which later became a farm known as Hewletts Farm.

73. Horfield Common, the north end, as it reaches the Gloucester Road, families and children enjoying the open space in May 1913, the path became Kellaway Avenue. Card published by Garratt.

74. Kellaway Avenue in the early years after its completion, in the early 1920's. The houses part of the new development in Horfield at that time. The wall and chimney of St. Ann's Cottage at the end on the right. A soldier exercising horses from the nearby Horfield Barracks.

75. A motor bus parked at the north end of Horfield Common. The card posted in February 1906, about the time when the buses were first introduced, replacing the trams. This bus was chain driven with solid tyres, destination Thornbury.

76. Horfield Common. A very rural scene with sheep grazing, one of the old rights of the common. The farm on the left Manor Farm. The houses facing the Common built in the early 20th century, are the same today, but the farm has been demolished for modern houses. Card posted in 1916.

77. Gloucester Road. A closer view of the houses on picture no. 76, shows they are well constructed bay villas, the bus a Greyhound, no. H.T. 2625. Postcard by Garratt and posted in 1923.

78. Horfield Barracks. A distant view with a solid wall surrounding it, next to the premises of the Duke of York Public House. The Post Office on the corner of Bayswater Avenue, selling apart from stamps etc., pure sweets, and picture postcards! Card published by Viner.

79. Gloucester Road looking from the common towards the city, the distant houses of Wellington Hill behind the car, the tram en route for Filton, the large house still has a verandah today. Card postally used in 1911.

80. Taken from the grounds of Manor Farm, towards the main road. Card published by Harvey Barton Ltd. and was posted on January 4th 1911.

81. Horfield. This view of the north part of Horfield Common opposite the Barracks, these men are recruits enlisting in 1916, they included men between the ages of 18-41 years, before then enrolment was only voluntary. The Duke of York Public House in the background.

82. Horfield Barracks with many recruitment posters on the wall. A delightful scene in 1910, with several modes of transport, and a group of children with baby in pram.

83. Horfield Barracks, as the gateways suggests, was built in 1847, and cost £57,000 to build, it was used by the Gloucestershire Regiment when this card was published in 1910.

84. Horfield Barracks, soldiers on parade, on a misty winter morning, the solid buildings within the barrack walls behind. In the past the Duke of Wellington visited the barracks on inspections, and is commemorated nearby in the naming of Wellington Hill, and the Wellington Hotel.

Horfield Barracks Church.

85. Horfield Barracks Church, set back from the road adjoining the barracks, next to the Duke of York Public House. The church is now converted into offices.

86. Horfield milkman Mr. Roberts, who lived in Boston Road, Horfield, and delivered in the local area, seen here with his son. His son didn't follow him into the dairy business, but worked for Bristol Aeroplane Company.

INDEX